We Left Constellations in Each Other

We Left Constellations in Each Other

Poems by

Whitnee Coy

© 2025 Whitnee Coy. All rights reserved.
This material may not be reproduced in any form, published,
reprinted, recorded, performed, broadcast,
rewritten or redistributed without
the explicit permission of Whitnee Coy.
All such actions are strictly prohibited by law.

Cover design by Shay Culligan
Cover image by Jennifer White
Author photo by Whitnee Coy

ISBN: 978-1-63980-783-3

Kelsay Books
502 South 1040 East, A-119
American Fork, Utah 84003
Kelsaybooks.com

*To Jesse, my gentle love—
I am endlessly grateful for the warmth and light you
bring to everyone's lives. We'd be lost without you.
I have no doubt that in every lifetime, in every
possible world, I will find my way back to you.
I love you.*

*For the lights of my life:
Ben, Elouise, & Sadie Miller.
I love you all more than words.*

*& to all those who've walked through the night with a NICU baby
—who have held their breath, held tiny hands, and held hope close.
This is for the brave hearts who choose to continue.*

Acknowledgments

Thank you to the following publications, in which versions of these poems previously appeared:

Alien Buddha Press: "Epiphanies After Divorce Papers," "The Separation," "It's Funny What People Will Say & Do to One Another," "sadie miller," "Meeting Again," "How Long Do You Visit?," "We Left Constellations in Each Other"
Choeofpleirn Press: "Lost Bugler Smoke"
Cypress Review: "Catching Up," "a year"
Fantasma: "Epiphanies After Divorce Papers"
Finishing Line Press: "Lost Bugler Smoke," "Open," "The Separation," "It's Funny What People Will Say & Do to One Another," "sadie miller," "Meeting Again," "How Long Do You Visit?" "Catching Up," "a year," "Settled Reality," "Clamoring Outsides," "Oral History"
Here Journal: "It's Funny What People Will Say & Do to One Another"
Highland Park Poetry: "Intertwined at the Root," "Open," "How Long Do You Visit?" "Fill Me Up," "First Marriages are Practice," "Years Later I Write"
Little Fish Magazine: "Settled Reality"
Women's Poetry Anthology: "Intertwined at the Root," "It's Funny What People Will Say & Do to One Another," "Social Worker Questions"
The Word's Faire: "The Separation," "a sky of bombs," "aubade for jc," "Fatherhood," "sadie miller,"

Contents

The Separation	11
Social Worker Questions	12
Oral History	14
How Long Do You Visit?	16
Swollen Marble Eyes	17
Clamoring Outsides	18
It's Funny What People Will Say & Do to Relate to One Another	21
Life from Death	23
Intertwined at the Root	25
Settled Reality	26
Plucked Pluck	27
Fatherhood	28
Meeting Again	30
Halloween	31
Stillness of Our World	33
First Marriages Are Practice Ones	35
Epiphanies After Divorce Papers	37
Years Later I Write	38
Open	39
a sky of bombs	40
Fill Me Up	41
Catching Up	42
a year	44
For Sadie Miller, on This Day	46
Lost Bugler Smoke	48
aubade for jc	50
We Left Constellations in Each Other	52
sadie miller,	54

The Separation

Before they pulled her wet-slicked being
from my numbed body, they prepped us:
we may not hear her cry.

Minutes before, her heart rate dived
to a faint tap & her 3lb body
had stopped moving.

No matter if I had changed position,
sipped chilled water, or however deep
they dug the ultrasound wand into me,

her life-filled body had become lifeless.

As my body rocked back &
forth like a swing in the wind, they
carved through 7 layers of my body.

I shivered from the coldness of metal
tools slicing thick tissue & the nurse
to my right gabbled everything
they were doing, reasons why, &

I couldn't hear a thing. Only thoughts of how
my 7-month-old baby that had grown a part of me
may not scream, cry, feel, or be alive.

My husband rested his hand
on my hairnet & soon we heard little bleats,
a wet lamb dropped in a pasture left to survive.

In a moment, we became two entities
left to laugh, wail, & feel the world's aches

separate.

Social Worker Questions

The night I was dying
my eyes were swollen shut as
the hospital bed's sheets
were changed repeatedly
from being soaked
in my urine & vomit.

The night I was dying
my nurse cradled my body
& held me, rocking me
in her chest as I cupped
my pregnant belly.

I didn't die that night.
Although white lab coats
scampered around my limp
frame like field mice.

Low voices hummed as if it were a secret
my body was shutting down. Turning off
the lights in each room
one at a time.

A month & a half later
in the NICU while holding my 3.5-pound
baby, a woman with a rusted-clamp clipboard nattered
about the weather, specifically the wind & gloom
as I had spent 4 hours in a room with no windows
holding the shell that was my baby.

Finally, she fumbled about what she was there
to ask: *How was I processing my near-death
experience & traumatic birth?*

I didn't know.

Just like I didn't know how many
ounces I had pumped alone & baby-less
being told to look at a photo of my daughter
in an incubator to try to squeeze
out more drops of milk.

I didn't know the last time I had brushed
my teeth or if my stitches had dissolved.
I didn't know when my baby would
or could ever breathe on her own.

I didn't know how I had spent days
in sterile hospital sheets & was expected to go home
without my baby & act as if the story were the same
because we had both lived.

How do I explain, all I did was spin
around the idea that the only thing
I had ever grown
had stopped moving the day I was dying?

Oral History

years to come
your red hair
will have wisps of silver,
like tinsels icing trees at Christmas
& everything will be a memory

your dad & i
long-gone snapshots
childhood floods you
at times, you least
suspect it.

you'll know you
got your dad's eye color
—an ocean clear with sun
sparkling on the riptides.
you'll know you
got my eye shape
—wide, half-dollar sized circles
left on check-out counters
in a Kentucky summer to pay.

you'll remember all
that has been told to you
over the years by those who love you.

mamie's pet spider monkey,
yellow-edged Valentine's Day cards tucked in
shoe boxes. siblings staggered on ladders to
look over the fence during COVID nattering
with neighbor kids. adoption papers found &

trees passed down to the tribe. Summer cabin
camping plans, Rathco concerts, board games,
dogs that never barked, dogs that always
barked, ripped trampoline nets,
the day you were born & we almost died.

How Long Do You Visit?

Her breathing on my chest
sounds like the slow release of a balloon
hissing after months of not
knowing how strong of a breather
she would be.

A hospital stay that long makes you tired
& confused & drifting in realities
where your baby is living outside your body
without you. You produce milk for no
one & days meld together & roll around
like marbles in a mouth.

People always want to know
how long you visit each day.
Like there's a sweet spot of time
that makes you a better mother
or father. The more time
drips by that you stare into a clear
box watching for chest movements of this baby,
a featherless, fallen bird.

If you say hours, there's an immediate pity
& confusion about how work
is letting you, or how your dishes
aren't sink-stacked, & how are your other kids
surviving? If you say about an hour,
there's a tinge of disgust
& a comment on how they could
never leave their baby
alone.

As if time were a testament to motherhood.
A testament to your womanhood.

Swollen Marble Eyes

There was a high
likelihood she would be still
born. Still, her heart
continued to whisper
as her body stopped moving
& my heart exploded.

I didn't cradle her to my freckled
chest or touch her for over 24
hours. In the panic of the room,
doctors didn't announce her sex
until a nurse asked
a few minutes later, she wiggled
on a cart, small chirps as
she was intubated.

Eyes swollen marbles, unopened
with blonde wisps of hair, a dream
I had never seen. Her red, wrinkled
limbs stayed in her plastic box,
with IV ports infused through toothpick
arms & purple-cut umbilical cord.

We'd visit her at night, when the
NICU daily rumbles were silent except
for the monitor beeps. Put our 3-minute
freshly washed hands into the box's
cut-out holes, room oxygen seeping out.
We rubbed her translucent skin
we never thought we would see
& forgot the ruckus
of the outside world.

Clamoring Outsides

living next to an elementary school
i'd hear the bells clamor
between periods, rushing sweaty
palmed kids in halls
to math equations, spelling bees,
& recess with broken swings,

as i waited in bed for the daily
doctor's call from the NICU.

last night was fine, not much
to report, no news is good enough
news, only one episode
where the nurse had to
help her breathe.

my breast milk was drying
no matter how many images
of the baby or videos i would watch of her
breathing with the help of a machine.
no matter how much fatty food or coconut-filled
drinks or maple-flavored supplements.
no matter how many hours or minutes
or seconds sat next to her clear box
watching her spindles for arms
with IVs, yellow & jaundiced.

the world charged on
outside of my pulled blinds
& the sucks and pulls
of a hospital-used breast pump
on my bedside for 45 days
was all i heard when
nursing a machine.

Unpacking Motherhood

I've never felt less like a woman
than when coworkers tried to explain to me
when my pregnant belly was as big as a globe,
how I would feel after my baby was born.
Women older than me & even a man
my own age, shaking his head in unison
with their chorus.

They tried to explain how everything would change
& while *I thought I would want to continue work, it would be*
    different & deep down I knew the same
was never told to my coworker, Ryan, when his wife
had their babies. Or how the explanation of
if I could balance it all // could work & yet
would I still be a good mom?
It was never the question to any of the men in the office.

It didn't make sense to me,
how I could be pushed into a box by people
who knew little of me; the surface // pond scum things.
The bits that float on everyone, we just assume
are the same. I had already been classified as hard to shift
as I would say no regularly, not engage in coffee cup
chatter, & kept things private.

Yet, because of societal expectations of motherhood &
the things their mothers did to them when they were young //
when forced to be latchkey kids, bopping around rides of
strangers, sneaking Virginia Slims from their mother's stash
    pressed into the deep lines of their minds

& worried them about the mother I would // could
be if I continued to work how I did.

The shape of women isn't created
by how well they bend
into boxes.

It's Funny What People Will Say & Do
to Relate to One Another

Her purple-hued legs, as long as my fingers
& the tubes that ran throughout her body
were as thick as her pine-needle arms.

When you explain to people
your baby is in the NICU, they never know what to say.
Prattle about a baby they once knew
who survived or read about
in a Facebook post. They preach phrases like "normal,"
"you'd never know," "even graduated early," or,
"only had a hole in their heart" to make you feel
relieved. Jostle, how lucky you are & how thankful
you should feel. Your baby will be *fine,* & these moments
will pass when you can't hold her, feed her, bathe her,
touch her petal-thick skin that you once grew.

Curious people ask if her eyesight
will be okay & I wonder if oxygen
lines will snake through her nose forever.
Or pry if she will always be so tiny—can she catch
up? All I can think of is that because she was born
so young, she hadn't learned the reflex of suckling &
swallowing. No matter how many breastfeeding articles
I read, it would never matter as a toothpick-sized
orange feeding tube winds through her nose
for nearly 45 days.

It's funny what people will say
& do to relate to one another.

When in the dark of night, while everyone rests
& IVs streak both of your arms, you cry
with no sound, so nurses or your husband don't hear
because you should be thankful you survived.
She survived.

But your body feels empty
& your arms pine to hold her
foot-long body next to yours in rough
patterned hospital sheets.

Instead, in the quiet beeps of hospital rooms
you grieve the dreams you had
for your pregnancy, birth, & the beginning
days of her life.

Grief is like heavy weights
tied to your feet as you learn to walk again,
shuffle one foot after another
to the NICU in the morning light.

Life from Death

My motherhood can't be disconnected
from my husband's fatherhood.

Just like the matching tattoos
we share show a permanent stamp
into our skins or how we knew
we wanted a child together
after our first date & spoke about our past
marriages & the past things that would always exist
& all the things we knew we could have only
if we spent the rest of our days
together & less than a year later

you sat sheltered in a hospital room,
leaned against a concrete slab wall
while experts rushed around
my bedridden body
believing I would die

& our baby would die.
Or, at best, you would be left
alone to raise her.

Your parents sprinted into town
in case the white coats were right
& you wouldn't be alone
if I never opened my eyes again
& if our baby never breathed
outside my womb.

But I didn't leave, although in moments
& minutes & hours during those days
I was an empty case of a human
floating out of consciousness.
In the days after, I had strangers
I couldn't remember who had been there,
taking my blood pressure or putting in a new
IV, who told me I was strong & a survivor.
They had witnessed my body swollen,
worried my body's fluid would
seep from my pores
while my liver shut down.

& all I could think about in the moments
of dubiety was that I had never
felt so alive than I had with you
& had never envisioned
death would look like the beginning
of the life that I grew.

Intertwined at the Root

They never tell you
that for the first six months of life
your baby has no understanding
that their little-limbed body
is no longer connected,
intertwined at the root
with yours.

They never mention to you
that your baby can't comprehend
that you don't feel their hunger,
as they squeal, lungs opening from the inside out.
Convinced they will never eat again & you
save them each time. They don't know their
whelps of fear with quivering bottom lips
& arms flinging out as you push
their toes into their onesie's feet
isn't as frightening to you.
That you understand they aren't
disappearing. Or that the heartbeat of yours
they hear, echoing in a silent vessel
of their body isn't their own anymore.
You can exist without one another.

How could you possibly expect her,
as delicate as a new web spotted
with rain after a summer storm,
to know so much
of this deep, wide, dark world?

Settled Reality

over 24 hours after she was
sawed from my body,
a limb outgrowing a weathered
tree; I was able to touch her
for the first time.

hands washed, scrubbed with
little plastic-bristle brushes
& a timer ticking away.

she wasn't pressed
wet & purple to my chest
like the movies
or the stories from friends
or the moments I had
envisioned months before.

instead, buttons pushed to calibrate
oxygen inside her container & given
permission to slide my fingers
nearly the length of her body,
skipping vessels & cords chartering
from her stomach, nose, arms, and head
keeping her alive. I sat wilted;
a crumpled shell in an open
backed hospital gown.

to lose something without losing

it can't be explained
but grief settles still the same;

light speckled dust on the top
no matter how much you clean.

Plucked Pluck

Pluck—(n) spirit and determined courage
(v) quickly or suddenly remove someone from
a dangerous or unpleasant situation

You are a girl made of pluck
plucked from the vessel of my body
ready to witness what the world
has to lay beneath you.

She's feisty, they would say
in the NICU as they laughed at the
nurse stations—& you were
& are. Your 2lb body, arms reaching outward,
legs at a 90-degree angle, you wailed.
Ribs moving as your sternum poked
beneath the surface of your thin skin,
a seedling ready to pop
in spring's soil.

The feistier the better, they reassured
& that would cross my mind when
her heart rate depleted
& oxygen levels would beep. Nurses
poking blue-gloved hands on her feet,
reminding her to breathe.

Her spirit remembered she was out
of the womb, no longer floating in
existence. Her body learning
how to live & survive in a world
not ready for her.

Fatherhood

To witness
you with our baby
tubes running like small
back-wood creeks
across the trunk of her body,
the size of your hand

heals the fatherless childhood I had.

A childhood
I didn't know
the difference
of never seeing a man
provide unwavering gentleness,
rooted like an oak tree.

Never knew how
a soft voice could fill
the spaces of a broken
body & addiction is not
woven into the fabric of masculinity.

Strength is quiet &
intentional &
dedicated & fills up
the room slowly,
an ocean reaching the shoreline bit by bit.

There was nothing
to compare & yet everything

rests on your shoulders
as your arms
surround her body.

You press her to your beating
heart, for 45 days
straight & I witness
what it means to crack yourself open
letting the light in
brightening other's shadows.

Meeting Again

At your dad's track meeting
with his students & their families,
the nurse who cradled
me as I was dying was there
with her family.

That night, she kept shaking her head
saying she didn't know what to do,
questioning why my body
was turning inside-out on itself,
after a healthy pregnancy.

She didn't recognize me
months later, as I didn't hold nearly 30 pounds
of swollen skin, ballooning
as my liver leaked blood.
I wasn't yowling from pain
in urine-soaked bed sheets.

When she hugged me
she held on tight
moving her hand over my shoulder
blades, touching reality.

She rocked my body,
the same she had that night

willing me to live.

Halloween

Nothing earlier than November.
The last comment chirped by a
doctor as I rocked my baby, in the stiff
NICU fake-wood chair. Her feeding
tube was freed that morning. She tugged it
out twice in one day, so they wanted to
Give it a shot & see.
She had been sucking
a bottle between choking
for the past 3 days
& we still had
7 days left of October.

3 days later,
a different doctor hummed,
She'd be home in 3 days.
I had never felt more
terrified as I still heard beeps
& witnessed daily her heart
& breathing rate drop like rain
outbursts on a spring day
before sudden silence.
Episodes, they noted them on
clipboards & digital charts.

She would be home on Halloween
& an already overflowing NICU
would continue the bustle of
saving babies, & our baby would
be home.

Monitor-less, choking still
after feedings, & a mere 5 lbs.

On a day of costumes & praising the dead
we celebrated in fear of the life
that would begin for a baby
already over a month old.

Stillness of Our World

Then the Lord God made a woman from the rib he had taken out of man, and he brought her to the man.

Unlike the Bible says,
you were not made from the rib
of a man & your existence
is not codependent on his presence.

But instead, you were made
in the promise of your parents
that we had never felt a love
like ours—deep rattling in bones,
yet gentle as night falls,
engulfing sunsets.

You, my girl, had no parts of others
that carried their way into you.
You are your own
& in that moment, you began,
a joining of things too small to see
but too big to understand
you had already broken any ideas
of what we could have hoped for.
What we whispered to one another
in quiet mornings, sunlight seeping
through blinds. What we had felt
when you would kick, pressing my stomach's
skin with the heel of your half-inch foot
We had chosen you & would choose you
in a thousand lives &

yet you would only be created
in this one.

We cheered with your start & rallied behind
not knowing how you would be,
even though some around us shared
their view of disappointment
but still celebrated your birth for all to
see. But that smallness doesn't
matter in who you are or who you
will become & all that you were
made for in the stillness of our world
you crashed into.

First Marriages Are Practice Ones

I read once at a tourist shop
on a magnet you'd see on an aunt's
white garage-refrigerator next to a
Hawaii sunset magnet her son
gave her 10 years before.
& as silly as it sounds, I believe it.
My first marriage hadn't quite been a year &
his mother strolled in on us bellowing
at each other across the broken-edge kitchen
counter strewn with tinsel & cracked lights.
Moments after, he announced he'd never
celebrate Christmas again.
I had made him hate it,
while slippery tears saturated my face.

To remember all the past times men lied,
twisted their words, & had made me fear
trust & companionship of anyone except
myself I'd be shoveling myself out of graves
dug for lifetimes & in that moment I knew
divorce was the only answer.

That night, we sat in silence for 45 minutes,
& soon our small, yet bulb-bountiful
Christmas tree stuck in a corner
between the tv & a small fridge packed
heavy with glass-bottom beers,
lights had fizzled out. The middle section
first, decorated with all my favorite

ornaments staring back at me became lost
in dark prickly branches of an
artificial tree.

I tried wiggling lights & unplugging
& soon the colored lights at the top
around the dull star-topper
silenced themselves.

Leaving us with a third-lit tree
& screams lighting the back halls
of our minds for months to come.

Epiphanies After Divorce Papers

Sometimes the best meat
is closest to the bone.
The deepest and hardest to peel
layers of tenderness from.

Sometimes the most a person
can say isn't anything
when there is nothing.
Silence—a ring spun around
a left finger or a wink only seen by two.

Sometimes there isn't a best,
good, or even alright.
At most there is remembering
you changed your socks
today, looked at your reflection, & to a fly you are
a soft, warm landing—for a large portion
of their short life.

Sometimes it doesn't matter how
sweet the taste, because there is still
a chance that it is too ripe. That the skin
is too delicate to snap
under the pressure of a bite.

Sometimes the end
doesn't quite feel like the end.
Instead, a broken carnival ride
set only to spin, a ship drifting
without a sail, a person left
alone in a house built for four.

Years Later I Write

When I was married to my ex-husband
I barely wrote & when I did
it felt like pulling my organs through
my throat one by one
still pumping
& wet.

I couldn't focus on poetry,
or metaphors, or the quiet little
moments that string humanity along
like christmas lights left up too long, a baby's
gummy giggle, dirty-sock pyramids
on the floor. I hadn't been touched for months,
or shared a bed, and even on days that felt
heavy yet ok, there was still
a sliver of a second, alone in the shower
or between the fogged-mirror wipes
I questioned why I thought life
was to be like this?

When did laughter molt
into nightly silent bathroom sobs,
and after 3 months of being wedded, my body
didn't feel like my own or it would just fold
on itself between his yells.

Years later, a new life, a new
family, a new baby, & a new
husband
who is gentle, & calm, & those
things I never knew I didn't have
is when I write;

the magic of things in hindsight.

Open

    Give me

                      your wide

                                      mouth,

            offing-like

                        and deep.

An ocean

                                    visible

                from land.

a sky of bombs

i can't help but think
how things would be different if she
came under sky-cascade of bombs
on the gaza strip,
explosions like the uncurling of broken
bones snap in the sky. images of starved
babies, four in one hospital crib
in darkness without electricity & running
water. their misshapen heads, ribs raised
through bodies like the flat & sharp
keys of a piano.

women, like Walaa, their bodies
inside out to give birth on the bitter cracked
earth between refugee tents with only her
uncle's wavering flashlight &
vibrations of bombs ricochet. no medical care
& a baby's limp purple body between her legs
waiting to be starved.

Fill Me Up

with all the water you can,
ballooning wide with all you had to
give that still wasn't enough.

anchor those hopes to my ankles clacking
around, a ghost of christmas past

let me sink to the bottom
of your mind's crevice
without the chance to float.

keep me locked,
keys hidden beneath sand
the sand of days before
and of ancient civilizations
rooted on the purest forms
of survival, forgiving the ripest better.

Catching Up

I've never been good
at math, the jumbling of numbers
of any kind, and yet

here I am, mentally subtracting
2.5 months from your actual age
at any given second to discover
your adjusted age—
a concept before you that
I never knew it existed. While you
exist in your actual age, white coats
until the age of two will only see you
as adjusted.

There was a period after you were born
when your doctors didn't even view you
as alive. There was nothing to compare
you to, a developing baby not yet on its
own. How could a baby, supposed to be
still in the womb, develop skills like
breathing and swallowing 10 weeks
early? Outside and disconnected from
life and still living?

November 26th, 2023
was supposed to be your birthday
& now on computer-typed forms
& certificates & conversations
or party invitations, it will always
say September 17th, 2023.

Your pediatrician, teary-eyed
thumbed through paperwork
to tell us after months
of tube feedings, syringes of medicine,
IVs, blood test pricks, eye exams
you had made it to the 3rd percentile
for your actual age.

You were finally alive.

a year

nearly 9 months alive
outside of the womb
& you said *mama*
lips pursed like a turtle's
& stood in your playpen
with sunshine radiating
behind your body.

on monday evenings,
when your dad & i share a beer;
a ritual we began between schedules, we
rock you in our favorite wooden booth as
you sip 8 ounces of formula,
eyes wide, looking at fellow regulars.

you can now wear a red-checked
flannel i wore when i was 7 months old,
yet still wear baby sandals, velcroed
straps made for those at 6 months of age.

5 bodies move through our home
exploding with baby toys, shaving cream slime,
empty dog food bowls, notebooks scribbled
with days of the week, dress-up costumes of
wild west outlaws, scraped-toe cowboy boots &
mud pieces tracked in from garden digs.

belly laughing, deep-voiced at 4 months
old, your 3 favorite furry friends made you
have gummy open-mouth smiles,
your full face shows 2 deep dimples.

in fewer months than i carried you,
you'll be 1 years old exploring a world
not ready for your early existence.

For Sadie Miller, on This Day

a year ago, you arrived,
a whisper of life in the sterile hum,
machines beeping blurts of
dropped heart beats while
sleepy-eyed parents shuffled
from stiff-furniture-filled
hospital rooms scattered
with empty cafeteria trays.

in those early moments,
when time held its breath,
you taught us to pause,
the heavy weight of now,
intentionality.

on your birthday, today,
you have belly laughs between
munches of mcdonald's salty fries
and totter in the park's autumn grass
without shoes. every chatter with your siblings,
interweave replacing the months
of monitors—heart rate, blood
pressure, breathing, the stopping of
breaths.

you licked icing off of a donut this morning
shocked to see "hey bear" banners
festooned and i think about how one time
in the starbucks line after a doctor's appointment,
you stopped breathing and i snatched you from

your car seat rubbing
your wax-like ears
as a reminder to breathe.

or the sleepless nights, sitting up in
shifts your father and i would take to
keep you propped on our chests, as laid
down flat in safe sleep you would choke,
turning blue-lipped. now you sleep in a crib,
a baby blanket made by a stranger
enveloping your 20 lb. body.

a reminder of how easily
things can change.

Lost Bugler Smoke

I've never seen an adult cry
like how I saw my grandmother
sob into my mother's shoulder
while clinging to a smoke-filled
quilt her mother
had made.

That day was long, moving
my grandmother & packing
her home of 19 years. Boxes perched
on shelves, watching us like roosted
owls supervising scampered field
mice. A home emptied into a house
as night overcame the sky
& settled thick
in the Kentucky summer air.

Near midnight,
we found ourselves
surrounding a rusted trunk
in my grandmother's bedroom.
She navigated the crooked
levers, releasing the top. Golden
aged pillowcases, once white,
protected precious hand-stitched
quilts. My grandmother sifted
through the colorful blocked
canvases of her mother, & of a time
when she was still alive. Twisted yarn poked
through each design, reflecting an
Appalachian way to quilt: hand tying.

In minutes, what smelled like a fire
burned our noses & filled the room
with haze. The three of us peered around
wondering what was happening
as the room filled with fog.

My grandmother
released her voice like an animal
caught in a trap, *"It's her. It's her cigarette
smoke. I've opened the trunk
& I'm losing her."* The trunk's top
slammed shut in between her inconsolable
cries. My great-grandmother's Bugler
tobacco smoke had filled the room,
seeping off the heirlooms released
from the opened trunk. My grandmother's
shoulders hunched, & her spine
poked through her shirt
with each earth-pulling cry.

Her wails, nothing that I had heard
& my own mother rocked her,
a boat trying to ride rough waves
through a storm. Soon, they both stood still,
& what sounded like the breaking
of bodies silenced in the haze.

We don't always know; the emptiness that
resides in a body not our own—no matter
how much we love & think we know.

We don't always know what will break us open.

aubade for jc

while light from outside snow
highlights your white-wired
beard hairs & speckle your dark
chest, i've never felt the warmth of
another & safety that hides
in the crook of your neck
waiting for me on this winter day.
any day / all days.

your lips are opened like the wrapping paper
on a christmas gift snuck early
beneath a droopy needle pine
& your glass-blue eyes flicker beneath
petal-like eyelids. the baby monitor
rumbles with soft-kid-snores & your heavy
breathing gives me a reason to know i
have searched 34 years for
a soft-edged/gentle/quiet/light/
morning love; not knowing you existed
in this light or bed or room or city.

i've been looking to find
a push my hair behind my ear for
me, matching initial tattoos at the kitchen
table on the second date, forehead kisses
when you think i'm sleeping during afternoon
naps, & late start mornings beneath sheets.
all i know is my body shakes itself
inside out beneath you & if that isn't
something then i don't know how anything
exists in this world. & yet

during this body-breaking
all is still & there's no noise,
idea, or being that could bring
me back to before
you & i existed together.

until this past december, i never
knew of the fusion of beings
or the existence of depending on another.
now it's here. in the quiet
that's not quiet & in the brightness
of light creeping through blinds.
there are interlocking fingers & legs, hair
spilling onto pillows, & sheet-covered torsos,
bent backs, crooks & crevices, & laid-on arms,
the delicate insides left out—
waiting to be picked
up by another in a world
built of alarm clocks, color-coded
schedules, & calendar pings.

instances of things we never
knew would breathe life into us
found in the early morning/
the stillness of light.

We Left Constellations in Each Other

It wasn't a red mirage
like Katie Couric assured me
via TikTok as I laid in bed between
my gentle husband & snoring baby,
bottle fallen from her lips,
positioned under a quilt my great-grandmother
had sewn, traced stitches with her own scarred
hands, labored over years before

her labor was recognized as much.
Tending to babies that weren't hers, years into
being an elder, making do with what they had, & fitting
into the hole society has punctured for her as a woman.
A woman who had been an unwed teen mom
with a baby from a local married man &
had married the older gentleman from towns
away to take care of his children
as his previous wife had died.

The juice is sour the next day.
The ripest of days are not to come
& I would be lying if I said I hadn't pictured
my redheaded baby motionless
on a dirty grout bathroom floor, pooled blood
& remembering the time, I miscarried myself.
With the assistance of doctors, able to keep living
after driving myself 1.5 hours
from work when my pants were blood
drenched after I taught.
But will Sadie Miller have the chance
to survive? Ectopic pregnancies, miscarriages,
sepsis, a baby that died in the womb,
all ways my baby can die.

I would be lying if I said I wouldn't teach my baby
if // when she is attacked to use her nails & scratch
for DNA. Or to carry her keys between her fingers.
Park next to light. To kick. Poke eyes. To deny getting
into police cars for speeding checks. Don't smile
when requested by strangers. & to understand it is still rape
even if she knows the man or even trusted him.
To bellow, "Fire" as "Rape" screamed is ignored
in both the literal & metaphorical sense.
That I want her to go toe-to-toe
with men & to never know how it feels to keep
returning even after purple-flowered bruises
blossom or you're dragged
over the couch by your hair.

That I didn't vote for a lying man
convicted of sexual assault
or who describes the pleasure
of shooting a woman,
but some of her loved ones did.

But for her to know that while it is clear
America does hate her
& loves the idea of her child body making a baby,
she is more than a vessel.
More than the 25 cents saved
on a loaf of wheat bread

or the thought of a gallon of milk
being cheaper. Her existence will forever be ingrained
in the old wood of my body, as our DNA
wrapped together as she grew in me

& together we left constellations in each other.

sadie miller,

you were named within an hour
on a cross-country road trip
as your dad zipped us
back from kentucky to south dakota,
a state i swore i would never return to.

things change & minds can change too
        //remember that when moments get hard &
        you worry about what happens
        if you learn more or grow & new possibilities
        look as sweet as blackberries
        try them//

on december 8th i knew things would never
be the same as i sat across from your dad
laughing so deep, i never felt more alive
or more like myself. every fear i knew
crumbled like dry leaves beneath feet.

    now watching you,
nearly 11 pounds at 5 months old,
you laugh fully. mouth extending,
showing mountains of pink gums.
dimples rippling over the pond of your face
        //always laugh fully, letting it take over
        the room, filling up spaces not originally made for
          you
        but you built for yourself//

your siblings cradled you
when they themselves were nothing but
children, & prayed your little 3-pound body

would live through the night your heartbeat
dropped. they practiced consoling their cousin's
baby dolls to be the best for you
        //love B & E always
        they will always be there for you//

don't forget that 912 franklin, our home,
is made of board games, art-lined walls, spilled
sodas, zach bryan's crooning records, kisses,
& pizza crusts left for dogs to eat.
it's muddy socks from trampoline jumps,
the best you can do on homework, heavy-gripped
hugs & hands held on couches piled with
extra blankets. there's always time
for naps, late-night television shows, belly laughter,
paint brushes left unclean, noah kahan stick-poke
tattoos, cat meows, stories of won recess-superbowls,
broken drumsticks, opened books, solved
math equations, empty drawn-on coffee mugs
& everything
in between.
        //remember, the best is found in the quietest of
           moments & times that feel messy. remember that
           love isn't linear
        or comes when you want it, but instead, at times,
           you need it.

        remember, you are the best of us we could offer
        & it still won't be enough for you//

About the Author

Whitnee Coy is an award-winning writer and educator living in the Black Hills of South Dakota with her husband, Jesse, and their three kids. She was raised by her single mother and grandmother in Lexington, Kentucky, where she attended the School for the Creative and Performing Arts (SCAPA) for Creative Writing and the Kentucky Governor's School for the Arts. Whitnee has her MFA in Creative Writing from Eastern Kentucky University's Bluegrass Writers Studio.

Three collections of her poetry are published, including *this deep, wide, dark world* (Alien Buddha Press). Her social-emotional learning children's book series *Elsie's Adventures* explores the neuroscience behind emotions and teaches coping skills for emotional regulation that can be done at home or in school.

A professor at Oglala Lakota College on the Pine Ridge Reservation, she also has her MA in Teacher Leadership with an emphasis in Secondary English and her Ed.D. in Education Policy, Organization, and Leadership, with an emphasis in Diversity and Equity, from the University of Illinois. When she isn't working or writing, she loves doing stick-poke tattoos with her husband and going to coffee shops.

About the Artist

The cover art for *We Left Constellations in Each Other* was created by Jennifer White, a contemporary Arikara artist and the visionary behind Post Pilgrim Art Gallery. Jennifer's work blends vibrant storytelling with Indigenous tradition, capturing movement, identity, and spirit. Her art holds space for layered memory—much like the poems in this collection.

Explore her work and vision at:
postpilgrimartgallerydotcom.wordpress.com/themastermind/

www.ingramcontent.com/pod-product-compliance
Lightning Source LLC
Chambersburg PA
CBHW070942160426
43193CB00011B/1778